AF228608

GREEK
MYTHOLOGY

POSEIDON

BY HEATHER C. HUDAK

CONTENT CONSULTANT
ALISON C. TRAWEEK, PhD
ADJUNCT INSTRUCTOR OF GREEK AND ROMAN CLASSICS
TEMPLE UNIVERSITY

Kids Core
An Imprint of Abdo Publishing
abdobooks.com

abdobooks.com

Published by Abdo Publishing, a division of ABDO, PO Box 398166, Minneapolis, Minnesota 55439. Copyright © 2022 by Abdo Consulting Group, Inc. International copyrights reserved in all countries. No part of this book may be reproduced in any form without written permission from the publisher. Kids Core™ is a trademark and logo of Abdo Publishing.

Printed in the United States of America, North Mankato, Minnesota.
102021
012022

Cover Photo: Shutterstock Images
Interior Photos: Photo Researchers/Science History Images/Alamy 4–5; SP Collection/Alamy, 6; Shutterstock Images, 8, 12, 16, 20–21, 22, 28 (top), 29 (top); Ali Kabas/Picade LLC/Alamy, 10–11, 28 (bottom); iStockphoto, 14, 15, 17, 18, 29 (bottom); Page Light Studios/Shutterstock Images, 24; Lena Yak/Shutterstock Images, 26

Editor: Alyssa Sorenson
Series Designer: Ryan Gale

Library of Congress Control Number: 2021941513

Publisher's Cataloging-in-Publication Data

Names: Hudak, Heather C., author.
Title: Poseidon / by Heather C. Hudak
Description: Minneapolis, Minnesota : Abdo Publishing, 2022 | Series: Greek mythology | Includes online resources and index.
Identifiers: ISBN 9781532196805 (lib. bdg.) | ISBN 9781098218614 (ebook)
Subjects: LCSH: Poseidon (Greek deity)--Juvenile literature. | Mythology, Greek--Juvenile literature. | Gods, Greek--Juvenile literature. | Sea gods--Juvenile literature.
Classification: DDC 292--dc23

CONTENTS

Poseidon's name means "lord
of the earth" or "husband of
the earth."

THE GOD OF THE SEA

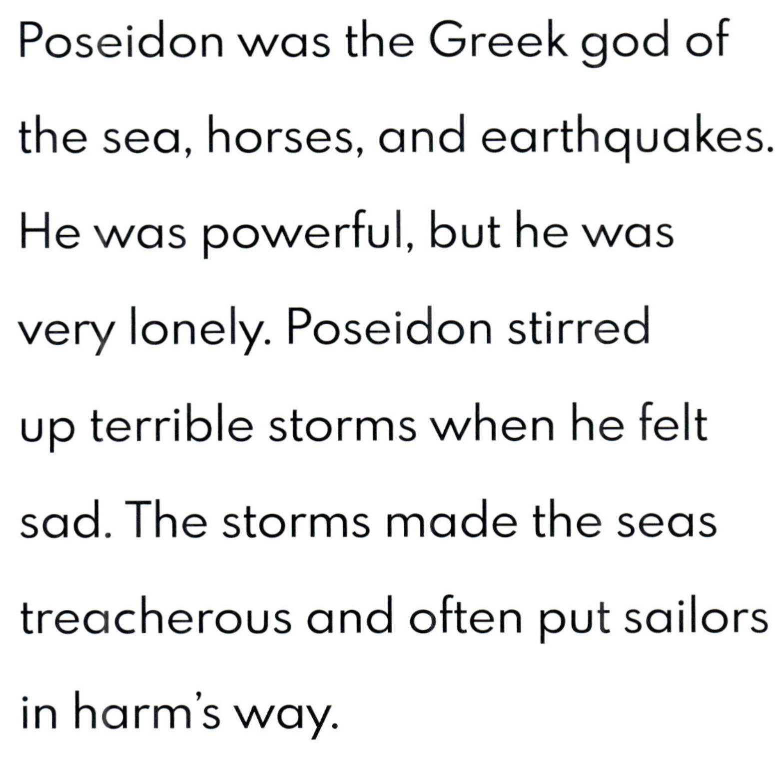

Poseidon was the Greek god of the sea, horses, and earthquakes. He was powerful, but he was very lonely. Poseidon stirred up terrible storms when he felt sad. The storms made the seas treacherous and often put sailors in harm's way.

Amphitrite is the goddess of the sea.

Poseidon wanted a wife to keep him company. He asked a sea **nymph** named

Amphitrite to marry him, but she said no. So Poseidon asked his dolphin-shaped friend Delphin to talk with her. Delphin told Amphitrite that Poseidon was sad without her. Delphin thought the seas would calm down if Amphitrite and Poseidon got married.

Amphitrite thought about it. She decided to marry Poseidon. To thank Delphin, Poseidon placed his friend among the stars. He became the **constellation** Delphinus.

God of Horses

There are many myths about how Poseidon became the god of horses. In one, the goddess Demeter asked Poseidon to make her a beautiful creature. So he made her a horse.

Greek myths include stories of monsters and the heroes who fought them.

Greek Mythology

Ancient Greece was a **civilization** in

southeastern Europe. It existed more than

2,000 years ago. Ancient Greeks often told

stories to explain the world around them. Some stories featured mighty gods and goddesses who had special powers. Others discussed heroes and monsters. These stories are known as Greek mythology.

People believed the gods would protect them from getting hurt. They also feared the gods would punish them for their wrongdoings. They prayed to keep the gods happy. One of these gods was Poseidon.

Further Evidence

Look at the website below. Does it give any new evidence to support Chapter One?

Poseidon

abdocorelibrary.com/poseidon

Artwork of Poseidon sometimes shows him with animals, such as horses or marine creatures.

CHAPTER 2

A MIGHTY OLYMPIAN GOD

Poseidon was the son of Cronus and Rhea. They were powerful gods known as Titans. Cronus was the king of the Titans. Poseidon had five siblings. His brother Zeus wanted to overthrow Cronus. Poseidon helped him.

Poseidon's Family Tree

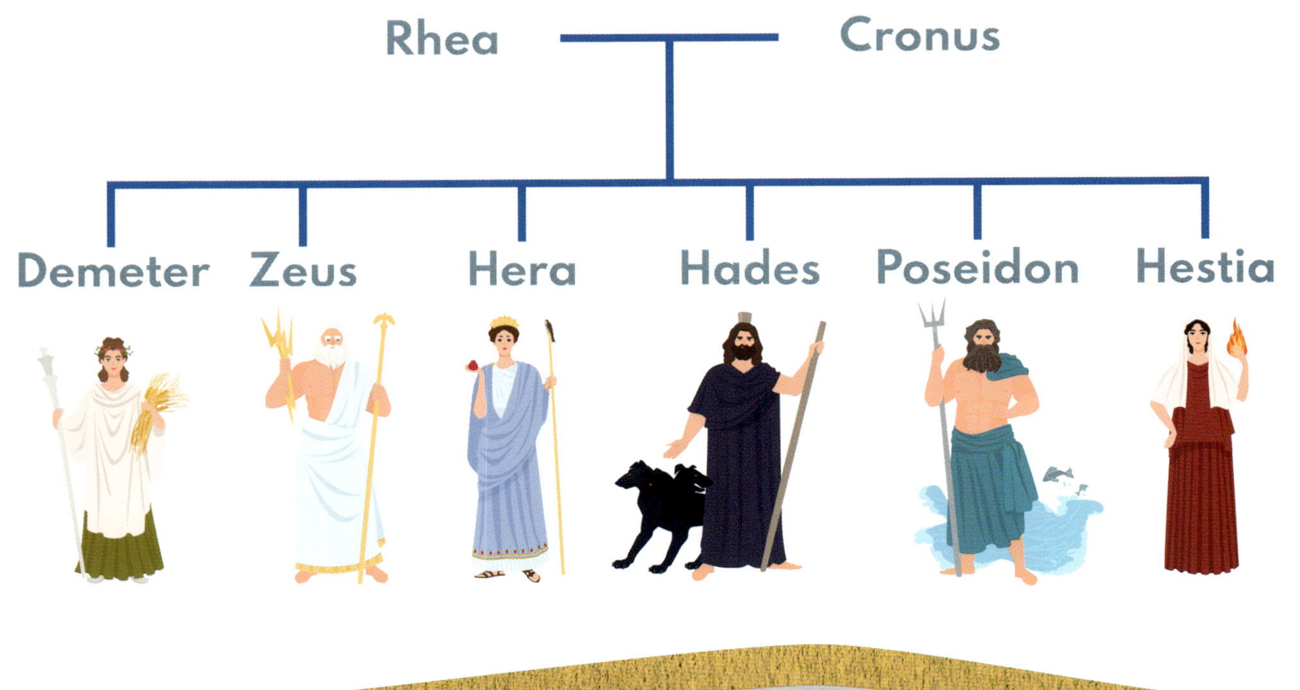

Poseidon had two brothers and three sisters. They were all gods and goddesses.

The war against Cronus lasted many years, but eventually Zeus's side won. Then Zeus became the king of the gods. Poseidon became the god of the sea.

Powers and Abilities

Many gods ruled from Mount Olympus. They were called the Olympians. Poseidon also had a palace at the bottom of the sea. It was made of gems, seaweed, shells, sand, and coral. He spent most of his time there.

Poseidon's Children

Poseidon had a few well-known children. Pegasus was a winged horse. Polyphemus was a giant cyclops. One famous story talks about what happened when the Greek hero Odysseus met Polyphemus. The cyclops imprisoned Odysseus. The hero had to hurt Polyphemus's eye in order to escape. Poseidon was angry about what happened to his son. He sent storms to wreck Odysseus's ship.

Poseidon had control over the sea and could make waves. He could also cause storms, floods, **droughts**, and earthquakes. He used his **trident** to shake the ground and shatter objects. He also used it to create or stop storms.

Poseidon had a bad temper. He was moody and unpredictable. He often got into **conflicts** with others. One time, Poseidon and the goddess Athena both wanted to rule over the same town. They competed for it. Each one gave the town a gift. The people in the town would decide which gift was better.

The trident was Poseidon's most powerful weapon.

Athena was Zeus's daughter. Poseidon was one of her uncles.

One story says Poseidon made a spring. But the water was salty like the sea. People could not drink from it. Athena gave the town an olive tree. The people could use it for oil, wood, and food. Athena won the competition, and the town was named Athens after her. Poseidon was very mad. He sent a flood to the area.

Another time, Poseidon and some of the other gods tried to take away Zeus's power.

Today, Athens is a large and busy city.

In one myth, King Cepheus tried to sacrifice his daughter, Andromeda, to Poseidon's sea monster. He wanted to make the god happy. A hero saved Andromeda before it was too late.

But Zeus could not be defeated. He punished the others for trying to overthrow him. He sent Poseidon and the god Apollo to work for King Laomedon in Troy.

Poseidon and Apollo built walls around Troy. The king refused to reward them for their work. Poseidon was mad. He sent a sea monster to destroy the city. It nearly ate the king's daughter.

Explore Online

Visit the website below. Does it give any new information about the Olympian gods that wasn't in Chapter Two?

The Gods and Goddesses of Ancient Greece

abdocorelibrary.com/poseidon

In artwork and statues, Poseidon is often shown as a strong, bearded man.

POWERFUL POSEIDON

Many parts of Greece are near the water. Ancient Greeks relied on the water for food and work. They prayed to Poseidon to treat them well and keep them safe. But people also feared him. Poseidon could make the seas stormy.

People today can visit the ruins of the Temple
of Poseidon.

Ships would sink and sailors would lose their way. He could even destroy an entire island with a tidal wave.

Ancient Greeks built **temples** to honor Poseidon. These buildings were often near springs, rivers, and lakes. One of the most important was the Temple of Poseidon in southern Greece. It was built on a cliff high above the Aegean Sea. People brought gifts to the temple. They thought the seas would be calm if Poseidon liked the gifts. The seas would be rough if he did not.

The Isthmian Games celebrated Poseidon. They happened every two years. People took part in sporting events. The winners were celebrated.

The Poseidon of Melos statue is made of marble.
It was created sometime between 150 and 100 BCE.

Portraits of Poseidon

Ancient Greeks made statues and paintings of what they thought Poseidon looked like. He is mostly shown as an older man with a beard. He often holds a trident. Dolphins, fish, or other sea creatures may be at his side. Sometimes he is shown riding horses through waves. The Poseidon of Melos is a large statue.

Percy Jackson and the Olympians

Percy Jackson and the Olympians is a well-known book series. It takes place in the modern day. The series is about a 12-year-old boy who is a son of Poseidon. He and his friends fight gods and monsters from ancient Greek myths.

It is at the National Archaeological Museum of Athens. It dates back to ancient Greece.

Poseidon is a big part of Greek myths. Many modern movies, video games, and books include stories of Poseidon too. People today are still fascinated by Greek gods and goddesses. They will continue to tell stories about Poseidon for many more years.

An unknown author once wrote about Poseidon. He praised the god of the sea:

> Hail, Poseidon, Holder of the Earth, dark-haired lord! O blessed one, be kindly in heart and help those who voyage in ships!

Source: "To Poseidon." *Perseus Digital Library*, n.d., perseus.tufts.edu. Accessed 20 May 2021.

Comparing Texts

Think about the quote. Does it support the information in this chapter? Or does it give a different perspective? Explain how in a few sentences.

LEGENDARY FACTS

Poseidon was the ancient Greek god of the sea. He was also the god of earthquakes and horses.

Poseidon helped his brother Zeus become the king of the gods.

Ancient Greeks made many paintings and statues of Poseidon. They also built temples and prayed to him.

Poseidon sometimes had a bad temper. He fought with other gods and with people. He would use the sea and the creatures in it to punish others.

Glossary

civilization
a society that's organized and developed

conflicts
fights, battles, or disagreements

constellation
a group of stars that form a pattern

droughts
long periods of time without rain

nymph
a divine female who lives for a long time and is connected to nature

temple
a building used for worship

trident
a spear with three prongs

Online Resources

To learn more about Poseidon, visit our free resource websites below.

Visit **abdocorelibrary.com** or scan this QR code for free Common Core resources for teachers and students, including vetted activities, multimedia, and booklinks, for deeper subject comprehension.

Visit **abdobooklinks.com** or scan this QR code for free additional online weblinks for further learning. These links are routinely monitored and updated to provide the most current information available.

Learn More

Flynn, Sarah Wassner. *Greek Mythology*. National Geographic, 2018.

Hudak, Heather C. *Zeus*. Abdo, 2022.

Menzies, Jean. *Greek Myths*. DK, 2020.

Index

About the Author

Heather C. Hudak has written hundreds of books on all kinds of topics. She loves to travel when she's not writing. Hudak has visited about 60 countries. She has been to many ancient sites in Greece that were built in honor of Poseidon and the other Olympians.